BITCOIN

MINING

MAKE MONEY WITH THE BITCOIN MINING
STRATEGIES. THE FUTURE OF BITCOIN.

THE 10 SECRETS TO SUCCESS WITH BITCOIN
ALSO FOR BEGINNERS.

BENJAMIN MYERS

written consent from the Publisher. All additional rights reserved.

The information in the following pages is broadly considered a truthful and accurate account of facts and as such, any inattention, use, or misuse of the information in question by the reader will render any resulting actions solely under their purview. There are no scenarios in which the publisher or the original author of this work can be in any fashion deemed liable for any hardship or damages that may befall them after undertaking the information described herein.

Additionally, the information in the following pages is intended only for informational purposes and should thus be thought of as universal. As befitting its nature, it is presented without assurance regarding its prolonged validity or interim quality. Trademarks that are mentioned are done without written consent and can in no way be considered an endorsement from the trademark holder.

TABLE OF CONTENT

Introduction

Bitcoin is an intangible currency, or cryptocurrency, which allows its holder to buy goods and services on the Internet or in real life. Unlike conventional currencies, Bitcoin, like all virtual currencies, does not have a central bank or any central body or financial institutions to regulate it. Instead, Bitcoin relies on a large over-the-counter network on the internet. Bitcoin is, in a way, the fruit of the marriage between the idea of a P2P network (over-the-counter), cryptography techniques, and the concept of money. Result: Bitcoin, and in its wake, other cryptocurrencies, maybe giving rise to a new kind of financial system, a completely decentralized, completely free alternative monetary system.

The underlying technology of Bitcoin is the blockchain or blockchain system. It consists of storing and transmitting data in a secure, transparent, and inviolable manner.

Each transaction is a block that is added to the others in an ever-growing chain of blocks that keeps track of all transactions.

This blockchain lives thanks to a network of computer nodes that makes it possible to use Bitcoin as a decentralized peer-to-peer digital currency. Any computer or device that connects to the Bitcoin interface can be considered a node. It communicates with other nodes by transmitting transaction and block information.

Bitcoin is the work of a genius who calls himself Satoshi Nakamoto. That's all we know. It could be a man or a woman. It could even be several people, no one knows.

You might be wondering how many Bitcoins there are in the world. At the end of 2019, around 18 million Bitcoins circulated in the world (compared to 16 million Bitcoins in 2016 and 10 million Bitcoins in 2013), for a money supply of about 66 billion, against 229 billion in 2018 (year of all records), $6 billion in 2016 and $1 billion in 2013. Thus, over 85% of Bitcoins are already in circulation.

To the question of how many Bitcoins are left to be mined, the answer is just under 3 billion.

The number of Bitcoins in circulation is automatically set

by a network of computer servers, called miners, scattered around the world. They take care of confirming

transactions and adding them to a decentralized transaction log. The volume of Bitcoins in circulation will reach precisely 21 million units in 2140. This is what the algorithm predicts.

A victim of its own success, the Bitcoin network, in its current configuration, will soon saturate, which risks be causing both traffic jams and degradation of service. Faced with this danger, a solution seems to be necessary: introduce technical innovations in order to allow the network to absorb more traffic.

Moreover, it was in 2017 to try to find an alternative that the fork took place, which gave birth to Bitcoin Cash, created from a secondary chain keeping a common core with the main blockchain. The latter makes it possible to validate the blocks of transactions carried out much faster, at a lower cost, but it also mobilizes a much greater computing power than that required by Bitcoin.

HOW ARE BITCOINS PRODUCED?

This is where it gets a little technical - and a little weird. Bitcoins are "excavated", following a predefined

algorithm.

They are found in lots of 25 units and reward the efforts of calculation aimed at finding the solution to what is very similar to a random mathematical problem. However, we are not talking about excavating or creating Bitcoins but rather about mining them.

Those who make Bitcoins are therefore called miners. The role of the algorithm is to ensure that the progress of the Bitcoin stock is slower and slower, halving the reward every four years. Thus, at the start of 2017, the reward fell to 12.5 units and then in 2020 to 6.25 units. At the same time, the level of difficulty of the mathematical problems to be solved increases over time, which has the effect of spreading the rewards.

The algorithm was designed so that Bitcoin behaves

exactly like a rare commodity whose exploitation offers diminishing marginal returns. A bit like gold or oil, for example (easy and cheap to find at first, then more and more difficult and expensive).

To mine Bitcoins, it takes more and more time and resources (computing power, hardware, developers).

Result: although virtual, the supply of Bitcoins is constrained. The algorithm thus gives Bitcoin immunity against inflation.

In this, Bitcoin is the complete opposite of the Linden dollar, the currency of the Second Life online virtual world (remember?). The latter is produced by a central authority, a de facto monopoly, at its will, without any limit.

The scarcity of Bitcoin is one of the elements that gives it value. Another element is its usefulness as a means of payment.

WHAT IS BITCOIN HALVING?

Bitcoin halving refers to the phenomenon by which the miners' reward is halved every 4 years or so, or every 210,000 blocks excavated. The last one took place on May 11, 2020, and two halvings had taken place previously: July 9, 2016, and, again before November 28, 2012. The halving of May 11, 2020, increased the miners' reward from 12.5 to 6.25 bitcoins.

Halving, due to the scarcity of Bitcoin it entails, tends to drive up the price of the cryptocurrency.

HOW TO MINE BITCOINS?

Perhaps you are tempted by the activity of a miner and you are wondering how to mine Bitcoins and above all, how many Bitcoins can you mine and in how long?

If the activity of miner could be relatively easy during thefew years which followed the launch of the famous

cryptocurrency, the computing power now necessary to mine Bitcoin is enough to discourage an individual from becoming a miner.

First, you will need to equip your computer with software intended to mine Bitcoin. Then, you will need to have enough computer equipment so that you can run your software while continuing to use your computer, which will not be easy.

Bitcoin miners are therefore above all professionals. They are even gigantic structures with substantial computer systems. In fact, Bitcoin mining has become more professional in recent years and Bitcoin is now mined in "farms", that is to say, warehouses of several thousand or even tens of thousands of square meters, housing server computers running at full speed, located in relatively cold

regions so that the servers do not overheat.

Bitcoin is experiencing unprecedented success in China, where there are no longer any mining farms for the famous cryptocurrency. Most Bitcoin miners are Chinese.

Thus, China's share in Bitcoin mining is estimated to be between 70% and 80% globally.

Bitcoins are used as a direct online payment method. However, they can be converted into dollars or euros on markets provided for this purpose. Physical coins have even been launched, which can be purchased online using either virtual Bitcoins or traditional means of payment, on eBay, BitMit, MemoryDealers, or even HardBTC.

HOW TO GET BITCOINS?

To obtain Bitcoins in a way that is both simple and fast, you have to resort to online platforms where you can buy them against euros or another currency (coinbase, binance...).

In most of these platforms, buying Bitcoins is done in three steps.

It is first necessary to open an account on the Bitcoin-Central site by creating a username and a password. It then becomes possible to fund this account in euros, or another currency, by bank transfer.

The user must then consult the site's order book. This order book lists the prices at which Bitcoin sellers are willing to exchange virtual currency for euros, or another currency.

Finally, you have to place an order by proposing a purchase limit price, which is the maximum price at which you are ready to buy Bitcoins. The order is only executed when a Bitcoin seller offers a price less than or equal to the buy limit price. Once the order is executed, the user's account is funded with Bitcoins and their holdings in euros, or other currencies, are transferred to the Bitcoin seller.

It is also possible to sell Bitcoins for euros, or other currencies, by placing a sell order. The euros in the Bitcoin-Central site account can then be transferred, by transfer, to a bank account.

Therefore, this means that a purchase of Bitcoins is not irreversible. However, beware of variations in the Bitcoin price, which may or may not be favorable to the user depending on the case.

HOW TO SPEND YOUR BITCOINS?

To pay a seller of goods or services in Bitcoins, it is necessary to receive from him an "address". An address is a succession of letters and numbers, to which the buyer sends the number of Bitcoins owed.

To receive this type of address, it is necessary to have a software wallet. You can install a software wallet on a omputer (with the Bitcoin-QT software for example) or a Smartphone (Bitcoin Wallet). The software wallet not only allows you to receive these addresses when you are a buyer but also, to generate them when you are a seller. Thus, each user must have his own software wallet.

Smartphone wallets can sometimes be used to pay in physical stores by simply scanning a code displayed on a screen. A very small number of stores, restaurants, or hotels accept bitcoin payments, but their number is steadily increasing.

There are also web wallets: instead of being installed on a specific computer, the web wallet is available online from any computer, subject to having the username and password. However, these wallets are much less secure than software wallets.

Bitcoin transfers, therefore, take place through this address exchange game: exchanging Bitcoins is comparable to exchanging emails. But, even more than for emails, it is crucial to secure your Bitcoin wallet, in particular through regular backups of your wallet.

A NEW USE OF BITCOIN: ICOS

The introduction of a company on the stock market is called, in English, an IPO (initial public offering). An ICO (initial coin offering) is a somewhat similar process, except that fundraising is carried out in virtual currencies, of which bitcoin is the best known, and that one does not acquire the ownership of a company. In most cases, this involves financing a new blockchain or an application based on an existing blockchain. This type of funding can be compared to crowdfunding in that the public can directly fund a bitcoin start-up. These ICOs operate in unregulated markets, resulting in increased risk for investors.

HOW ARE BITCOINS CREATED?

Buying on platforms provided for this purpose is not the only way to get Bitcoins, although it is simple and fast. Indeed, Internet users can also participate in the process of creating new Bitcoins and the authenticity of the payer and the availability of funds must be obtaining them as well. This is called "Bitcoins mining".

A new user who wants to be content with just buying Bitcoins through the planned platforms does not need to know how Bitcoins are created.

To ensure the credibility of the system, it is necessary that the authenticity of the payer and the availability of funds are verified when paying in Bitcoins. This is why a monitoring process is put in place: in concrete terms, Internet users who are members of the network - the "Bitcoins miners" - invest in computer equipment that they make available to the system for its proper functioning and security. The computers of these Internet users are then put in competition to develop complex mathematical functions which make it possible to verify the validity of the transaction. The one who wins the validation is rewarded by receiving newly created Bitcoins.

HOW TO SPEND BITCOINS AROUND THE WORLD?

Once your Bitcoins have been purchased through BYKEP and your tobacconist, you are probably wondering how to spend your Bitcoins to buy goods and services like with a regular currency. With the gradual adoption of Bitcoin around the world, it now seems easier and easier to use your Bitcoins to buy goods. Remember that Bitcoin is not intended to be an object of speculation, but a global currency.

At the time of the first Bitcoin transaction, almost 10 years ago, it was still very difficult to buy goods with Bitcoins, the situation has changed a lot since then. While not all points of sale accept Bitcoin payments, the adoption is underway.

The best example is the possibility of paying in Bitcoin on Amazon and soon on Domino's pizza. Starbucks is also considering whether to accept bitcoins. Even Italian supercar maker Lamborghini has taken to Bitcoins.

There are also solutions to use your bitcoins indirectly, through conversion into a national currency. This is made possible by the many exchanges like Coinbase or Binance. Recently, we have also seen initiatives appear to allow you to use a bank card directly linked to your Bitcoin wallet. Coinbase has just launched its card in Europe, the companies Wirex and Monaco have developed similar projects. Finally, many sites allow you to buy Bitcoin gift cards, the vouchers purchased then giving access to a wide range of products and services. These sites are for example egifter; Gyft and purse.io.

Let's take a look at the sectors that stand out in the adoption of Bitcoin as a payment method in its own right.

E-commerce:

In the white paper behind Bitcoin, founder Satoshi Nakamoto already spoke of the development of e-commerce as one of the factors explaining the creation of a completely digital currency. It is therefore understandable that some major players in the sector are positioning themselves favorably and accept Bitcoin. Here are some examples.

Amazon: The most famous e-commerce platform, which offers almost everything for sale, accepts payments in Bitcoin! This is excellent news that will undoubtedly push traders to adopt cryptocurrency.

Overstock: it is a company that directly accepts payments in Bitcoins. On this site, you will find furniture, televisions and even computers.

Newegg: This online electronics merchant accepts Bitcoin payments on most of its stock.

Video games:

The video game industry, as seen by Ubisoft's latest announcement developing a blockchain project, is a ripe industry to embrace cryptocurrency payments.

Xbox: Here you can buy premium games and subscriptions to the online network.

PlayStation Network: Available for PlayStation games and subscriptions.

Zynga: The creator of online and mobile games also accepts Bitcoin.

The tourism sector:

Competition is very strong in the field of travel booking sites. Accepting Bitcoin is a good way for sites to differentiate themselves. We thus find many actors for example:

Expedia: This is one of the biggest tourists booking sites in the world, you can spend your Bitcoins to buy plane tickets, book a hotel, an excursion, or even a rental car!

Virgin Galactic: If you want to buy your ticket for space in Bitcoin, it is possible! Richard Branson's company accepts Bitcoins well.

Air Baltic: The first airline to offer flights payable in Bitcoin.

IS BITCOIN A REAL CURRENCY AND A REAL MEANS OF PAYMENT?

It is a vast quasi-philosophical debate, but we will try to provide you with some avenues for reflection.

To be a widely accepted means of payment and a store of value, the currency must be an object with the following properties: non-perishable, identifiable, difficult to counterfeit, easy to transport, easy to store, fungible, and divisible.

Let's see if Bitcoin has these properties:

- Non-perishable: obviously yes.
- Identifiable: like banknotes, each Bitcoin has its own number. So yes, well identifiable.
- Difficult to Counterfeit: Impossible to counterfeit, but a person with enough computing resources might try to use the same Bitcoin to make multiple payments.

- Easy to Carry and Store: As long as you have a smartphone or a computer, it is easy to store and transport a large number of Bitcoins.
- Fungible: In the same way that a gold bar is interchangeable with a gold bar, a Bitcoin is interchangeable with another Bitcoin. It is therefore quite fungible.
- Divisible: a Bitcoin can be subdivided into 100 million units, called satoshis

At first glance, Bitcoin has all the properties of a currency. But that does not guarantee its success. Indeed, to be successful, a currency must inspire confidence and, above all, be useful. The two are also intimately linked.

To inspire confidence, Bitcoin must intimately convince its users that they will be able to exchange their Bitcoins for goods and services at any time.

The users of a currency are part of a vast exchange network, and the value of this network increases due to the number of people who compose it. To be truly useful, Bitcoin must therefore be accepted by enough people.

Bitcoin, like all currencies, has an abbreviation (EUR for Euro, CHF for Swiss Franc, etc.). It is often designated by the abbreviation BTC but we also find the abbreviation XBT to speak of the first of the cryptocurrencies. This financial name, even if it is not official, corresponds to the system in force on the financial markets. Thus, in "XBT", "BT", corresponds to the abbreviation of Bitcoin while the "X" located in front reminds us that this asset does not belong to any country as is the case of the "X" in "XAU" which designates gold.

WHAT CAN YOU BUY WITH BITCOIN?

Several states have officially recognized Bitcoin as a method of payment, such as Japan in March 2017. In fact, cryptocurrency is very popular there and Bitcoin payments are relatively common. However, this is not the case everywhere in the world.

In France, few traders accept to be paid in Bitcoin. Most of the businesses that accept it are on the Internet. Overstock or Shopify merchant sites, in particular, accept payment in Bitcoins. The WordPress blog platform also accepts Bitcoins. But there are also a few physical stores in which to spend your Bitcoins. Please note, in France, they are almost all located in Paris.

It is, therefore, possible to buy computer hardware, software, and IT solutions, but also everyday consumer products such as furniture, decorative objects, clothing, etc. You can either buy Bitcoins by exchanging a currency (euro, dollar, etc.) for Bitcoins, or you can offer a good or service for sale by setting its price in Bitcoin.

In any case, you will need to create a cryptocurrency wallet to be able to hold your Bitcoins. The question of the famous wallet then arises. Which Bitcoin wallet to choose from? Which site to favor to hold Bitcoins? The question is far from trivial given the hacks or bankruptcies that have affected many players in the sector.

To keep your Bitcoins, you must have a wallet, that is to say, an address in the form of a series of digits that can be accessed using a password. Address and password can be created for free and easily on a dedicated platform.

However, to pay or receive a payment in cryptocurrency, you will need to either download software or use an exchange platform.

Finally, to pay with a cryptocurrency (or receive a payment in cryptocurrency), an intermediary is necessary. You will have the choice between an exchange platform similar to a broker or software to download.

HOW TO PAY IN BITCOIN?

There are three ways to pay in Bitcoin, whether the transaction is for the purchase of a good or service.

First, you can use the QR Code provided by the seller. All you need to do is scan it with your smartphone which will automatically open your Bitcoin wallet application.

You will then only have to validate the payment by first checking the sending address of the sum and the amount.

But you can also pay an online merchant on your computer and click on "pay in Bitcoin". In this case, your wallet will open automatically. Again, you will need to verify the recipient's address and the amount before validating your payment.

Finally, you can also choose to send a payment manually. You will then have to open your online wallet and copy the merchant's address into the "send to" or "recipient" field and specify the amount in XBT of the transaction before sending your payment.

WHY BUY BITCOIN?

As we have seen, Bitcoin payments are relatively limited and few merchants still accept to exchange the goods or services they offer for sale for Bitcoin. So, why invest in

Bitcoin? What is the interest in Bitcoin? How is Bitcoin increasing in value? Why has Bitcoin exploded? Here we

explain the reasons to buy Bitcoin and how to make money with Bitcoin while keeping in mind the risks.

Admittedly, Bitcoin can be exchanged all over the world, via any computer or smartphone, without any bank intermediary since specialized brokers are responsible for converting bitcoins into classic currencies, including the euro and the dollar, and this makes it an international and independent means of payment. Cryptocurrencies represent an alternative means of payment based on the blockchain with all the advantages that this implies (traceability, security, etc.) and this constitutes an undeniable advantage. However, this is not the only reason for the surge in prices.

Then, let us emphasize that Bitcoin can play the role of safe haven in the event of a crisis and in countries whose currency is frequently subject to devaluation. Thus, the Chinese government's policy of controlling the outflow of capital from Chinese nationals and the continued decline of the Yuan largely contributed to the success of Bitcoin in the Middle Empire.

Consequence: three Chinese platforms, Okcoin, Huobi, and Btcchina, have captured more than three-quarters of global Bitcoin volumes since 2016. Some even speak of Bitcoin as a Chinese currency.

But if Bitcoin is so popular, it is above all thanks to the prospect of realizing a significant and rapid potential capital gain. Indeed, the craze that exists around the precious token is above all based on speculation without the intrinsic value really entering into account. It must be said that the volatility of Bitcoin and its significant rise in the long term is enough to make traders dream.

HOW TO INVEST IN BITCOIN?

Despite its very geeky image, in September 2015, the regulator of the commodities market in the United States, the Commodity Futures Trading Commission, officially declared that Bitcoin fell under the commodity category.

It is therefore the first step towards the regulation of virtual currencies and a certain recognition of cryptocurrency by financial institutions.

Financial transactions in Bitcoin and trading on

specialized platforms must now be carried out in accordance with the rules governing the exchange of raw materials.

There are plenty of web platforms that offer bitcoin & cryptocurrency investment, the further sections of the book explain the steps which can be performed on any of the crypto trading website mentioned below:

- Coinbase (https://www.coinbase.com/)

- Gemini (https://www.gemini.com/)

- BlockFi (https://blockfi.com/)

- Kraken (https://www.kraken.com/)

- Robinhood (https://robinhood.com/)

- eToro (https://www.etoro.com/)

- Bitcoin IRA (https://bitcoinira.com/)

- Binance (https://www.binance.com/en)

But we are also witnessing the emergence in the United States of trust companies specializing in cryptocurrencies such as LLC and IT bit.

These two companies, in addition to meeting New York State Department requirements for capitalization, reserve, compliance, consumer protection, and cybersecurity, also provide warranties for computer storage systems and security systems. Cold storage vault for Bitcoin holdings from the famous GABI fund. The manager of the GABI fund offers the possibility of exchanging these particular transferable securities into Crypto Delta One (CRYDO). CRYDO, therefore, makes it possible to trade its securities on an electronic trading platform that offers indirect or synthetic exposure to the underlying price of Bitcoin without transmitting the explicit ownership of Bitcoin.

Bitcoin is becoming a separate financial product!

Now is the time to invest? One can indeed wonder when to invest in Bitcoin. If you want to invest in BTC, go for it. Perhaps you think it is too late given the already high price of crypto, or that it is still a bit early because it has a relatively low penetration rate in the real economy. Avoid looking at your investment from a market timing perspective.

It is impossible to predict the price of this hyper volatile asset and at what level the prices of BTC will be in a month, in a year, and even less in 2. If you are tempted by the adventure and want to invest in XBT, do -the. But by diversifying your investments and using the money you don't need.

Are you wondering how to invest in Bitcoin in France? And where to invest in Bitcoin, via which platforms and which brokers? To invest in virtual currency, two solutions are available to you: invest directly by exchanging euros for Bitcoins via specialized platforms such as Poloniex, Circle, or Coinbase. You can also speculate on Bitcoin via financial products derived from the most famous virtual currencies. Several online brokers offer CFDs on Bitcoin. Indeed, online brokers eToro, IG, or even XTB allow you to invest in Bitcoin through a CFD on electronic money. Be careful, before putting your savings in cryptocurrency, ask yourself how much to invest in Bitcoin. Measurement is necessary when it comes to investment and the diversification of one's holdings remains an essential factor in the sound management of a portfolio.

Especially since Bitcoin is a particularly volatile asset! You will therefore have every interest in investing only the pennies that you can afford to lose. In addition, the use of derivatives and leveraged products will be recommended to the most sophisticated investors, who will be able to fully understand how these products work and the risks involved. Recall that 89.4% of retail traders lose money according to the Study of results of retail investors on CFDs and Forex trading in France carried out by the Autorité des Marchés Financiers on the basis of the results obtained by nearly 15,000 French private traders from 2009 to 2013.

HOW TO SELL BITCOIN?

For Bitcoin investors who have chosen to position themselves on live BTC, without going through the derivatives of a stockbroker like eToro, which provides liquidity allowing the investor to sell his Bitcoins at any time, it is crucial, when you want to get out of your position and make a possible profit knowing how to sell BTC. You can first sell your Bitcoins on an exchange platform like Kraken, Coinbase, or even Bitstamp.

After choosing your platform (pay particular attention to special fees and conditions such as a minimum deposit) and creating your account, you can place a sell offer indicating the currency in which you want to collect your funds. As soon as someone is interested in your offer, the platform will automatically carry out the transaction. You can then transfer the money to the bank account entered during registration.

It is also possible, but it is much rarer, to be able to sell Bitcoins via a physical exchange platform such as Coinhouse in Paris or certain Bitcoin ATMs (more present in Asia). You will need to bring your identity document and your smartphone to send your XBTs to the wallet of the physical platform via a QR code. You will then receive your euros in cash or by transfer.

You can also sell your Bitcoins directly to another person as long as they already have a wallet. To sell your XBTs, all you have to do is scan a QR code that will allow you to send the sold Bitcoins to the buyer's bitcoin wallet, all in just a few seconds.

HOW DO I KEEP BITCOINS SAFE?

After you have bought Cryptocurrencies on an exchange, your balance is managed by this exchange. The bitcoins belong to you but are in the account of the exchange, the so-called wallet. In the past, exchange wallets were the main victims of attacks. It is therefore advisable to transfer the bitcoins to a personal wallet. You get the unique code of your coins. Save this on several devices. These devices should ideally be offline. But note: if you lose the code, your money is gone too.

As the price of bitcoins continues to rise, so does the interest of hackers. The blockchain itself is secure, but not always the personal computer. Here's a comparison: The Swiss franc as a whole currency is very difficult to manipulate. But that doesn't stop pickpockets from stealing a note from your wallet. Your bitcoins are only as secure as your virtual wallet. That is why there is now insurance for cryptocurrencies. Your crypto money is also insured within the Safe Pay cyber insurance from Basler

Insurance. So, if someone misuses your data, gains access to your wallet, and transfers your crypto money, Baloise will compensate for this financial loss up to CHF 20,000.

SELLING BITCOINS AND PAYING WITH BITCOINS

Bitcoins are also sold on the stock exchanges. This is very easy, for example, via BitPanda. Here you just register with your own email address. You can choose to pay out via instant transfer, PayPal, or Amazon vouchers. BTC direct works without registration. The amount is paid out via bank transfer. Bity manages a very quick payout; sometimes you get the money on the same day. The exchange even offers coin ATMs at various locations in Switzerland.

As mentioned, Bitcoins are not a stable means of payment at the moment. Nevertheless, you can also pay with cyber currency in certain shops in Switzerland and even at SBB ticket machines.

A transaction directly between two wallets is made possible via QR code and the crypto wallet app. After the transaction is confirmed by miners, the buyer's and seller's wallets are adjusted. This check takes about ten minutes.

Thank again for choosing this book make sure to leave a short review on amazon if you enjoy.
I'd really love to hear your thoughts.

Chapter 1
Cryptocurrency

Since the introduction of the euro, we Europeans have got into the habit of going on vacation abroad without taking into account exchange rates and other local monetary specificities. And yet, this is not the case for everyone: everywhere outside Europe, the slightest border crossing entails unwanted costs, and we often end up with unusable tickets in the back of our pockets when the trip is over.

The alluring idea of a universal currency has certainly been around much longer than the euro, but it is only recently that we have witnessed the birth of a real prototype: Bitcoin. However, many questions arise. Can Bitcoin Be A Global Currency? What about other crypto assets? On what criteria to judge crypto-currencies? Or, what will their future be?

To answer it, we will have to observe the birth of Bitcoin as well as its precursors, but also the development of the entire current crypto-asset ecosystem.

Then, we will study the nature and philosophy of crypto-currencies in general in order to reflect on the issues encountered in 2018.

By cryptocurrency is meant both a cryptographic currency and a peer-to-peer payment system. These digital currencies are therefore virtual currencies in the sense that they are characterized by an absence of physical support: neither coins nor banknotes and payments by check or bank card are not possible either.

These are alternative currencies that are not legal tender in any country in the world. Their value is not indexed to the price of gold or to that of traditional currencies, nor are they regulated by a central body or financial institutions. There are no central banks at their head. And yet, security and transparency are their main assets! Because in fact cryptography secures transactions that are all verified and recorded in a public domain, ensuring both confidentiality and authenticity thanks to Blockchain technology.

BLOCKCHAIN: THE BASIC TECHNOLOGY OF CRYPTOCURRENCY

Cryptocurrencies are all based on the same principle: the Blockchain. Cryptocurrencies are a series of numbers stored on a computer in the form of chains of blocks. The principle is actually quite simple and particularly well explained in the section published in Les Echos *Bitcoin and cryptocurrencies, new digital coins*: "Take a database. Allow anyone to make changes to this database, on the sole condition of declaring themselves a "member". Set up a very long and very complex control procedure which must be carried out each time a certain number ("block") of changes is requested. This procedure is carried out not by a single controller, but by all the voluntary "members". Once validated, the "block" of changes is dated and added to the others in the registry. Finally, let everyone read the registry, and you have a blockchain database". Thus, it is up to the network (all the peers) to validate and confirm each transaction.

This technology and this system are the basis of the vast majority of cryptocurrencies, but Blockchain applications do not stop there. Indeed, it could disrupt the entire financial sector but also certain sectors such as the legal or administrative sector by eliminating the need for trusted third parties. No need for a notarial act or civil status register or even cadaster with this distributed register technology which helps to make data more secure and transparent. Blockchain technology is after all a technology whose database cannot be changed without meeting certain conditions.

HOW IS CRYPTOCURRENCY MADE?

People who make cryptocurrency are called miners. It is also said that they mine a cryptocurrency. Minors are an integral part of the process. Without them, the Blockchain would be frozen. **A miner in fact confirms the transactions that take place on the Blockchain.**

For example, imagine that Peter gives 3 Bitcoins to Paul. The transaction will be immediately broadcast on the network, peer-to-peer, made up of computers called nodes. However, it is only after a certain period of time that the transaction will be confirmed by the computers belonging to the networks using the algorithms specific to said Blockchain. Once committed, the transaction now forms a new data block for the ledger. It is added to others in the existing Blockchain, permanently and immutable.

Behind these computers on the network, miners validate transactions. To confirm a transaction, a miner must find the product of a cryptographic function that connects the new block to its predecessor.

This is called proof of work. In exchange for their services (and the computing power mobilized for this purpose),

they obtain a reward that takes the form of tokens or tokens.

HOW TO MINE A CRYPTOCURRENCY?

To undermine a cryptocurrency, it is usually sufficient to install software on your computer using the processor or the graphics card, or even both, in order to be able to solve the cryptographic problem requiring a relatively large calculation power, which will allow you to touch new units of the cryptocurrency in question. Be careful however, the main cryptocurrencies have become too difficult for individuals to mine. The mining of many of them has become largely professionalized and takes place in part on Chinese farms, buildings of several thousand m2 where tens of thousands of servers run day and night to mine cryptocurrencies (Bitcoin, Litecoin, etc.).

Faced with this competition, cloud mining solutions have been developed. No investment in specific hardware is required. All you have to do is get in touch with a company

that has invested in the necessary equipment and "hire" your computing power. But beware, there are many scams!

WHICH CRYPTOCURRENCY TO MINE?

Obviously, individuals are keen to mine the most profitable virtual currencies like Bitcoin, but also Dash, Ethereum, Monero, Litecoin, etc.

However, it is very difficult today to make money by mining a cryptocurrency. It is often much more interesting to invest in virtual currency in order to hope to make profits.

MINER / DEVELOPER: WHO MAKES THE CRYPTOCURRENCY?

The role of the cryptocurrency miner is therefore to validate the transactions carried out. He is thus paid in tokens of the cryptocurrency for which he has confirmed a new block. The role of the developer is very different. A cryptocurrency developer will develop the computer protocol at the base of the cryptocurrency which defines, in particular, the number of tokens in circulation, their speed of circulation, their storage power, etc. He is somewhat the architect of the network.

BITCOIN, ETHEREUM, RIPPLE: THE MAIN CRYPTOCURRENCIES

How many cryptocurrencies are there? This often-asked question sounds simple but in reality, it is very difficult to know the exact number of virtual currencies. No site lists them all.

The Ministry of the Economy and Finance counted more than 2,871 in 2019, without having carried out an update since. There could be nearly 3,000 today, but that's not the most interesting thing. It should be noted that there are very many cryptocurrencies but that only a few dozen can be qualified as popular cryptocurrencies.

We often tend to rank promising cryptocurrencies based on their market capitalization, and rightly so.

The cryptocurrency Bitcoin, created in 2008 by Satoshi Nakamoto (without knowing who he is, whether it is a man or a woman, or even a single person or several) is the first of cryptocurrencies. He is somewhat the digital gold standard of the cryptocurrency sector, the benchmark in the field. The main cryptocurrency experienced a "fork" in August 2017. A disagreement in the Bitcoin community over the speed of transactions gave rise to the birth of a new currency: Bitcoin Cash, which immediately rose to the third position in the Top 10 cryptocurrencies and has held its own since then. in this Top 10.

Indeed, in parallel with Bitcoin, there are many other cryptocurrencies such as Ethereum for example, which also experienced a "fork" in the summer of 2016. Ethereum, more complete than Bitcoin, is based on all Blockchain applications since it can not only process transactions but also complex contracts and programs. We can also mention Ripple which is not only a cryptocurrency (XRP) but also a transfer system operating independently of the XRP token.

It is above all a digital payment protocol intended to facilitate interbank payments. Litecoin, Cardano, NEM, Monero, Stellar, or Iota are also cryptocurrencies that are regularly part of the 10 most important crypto-currencies. Since the creation of Bitcoin by Satoshi Nakamoto, around 3,000 crypto-currencies have emerged. It should be noted that cryptocurrencies are numerous, that new ones can emerge and challenge the heavyweights of the sector, but also that disagreements within a community can lead to a "fork" (fork in French), that is to say, a split within the community and the creation of a new currency based on the technology of the old but with modifications.

CRYPTOCURRENCY PRICE OF THE DAY

If the coronavirus crisis has also impacted the price of crypto-currencies which have experienced a massive drop since the confinement of populations in the hope of stemming the Covid-19 epidemic, they largely caught up at the end of the year. year. The Christmas rally of Bitcoin and other virtual currencies in its wake has been impressive, to say the least.

In this troubled context, cryptocurrencies have finally succeeded in establishing themselves as a safe haven. As Nathalie Janson, Economist and teacher-researcher at NEOMA Business School underlined at the beginning of December 2020: "radical economic uncertainty, negative rates, weak dollar" are all factors that contribute to the rise in the price of cryptocurrencies.

Bitcoin, which set a new record at over $40,000 at the start of 2021, leads cryptocurrency in terms of market capitalization.

Recall that the price of Bitcoin is only partially correlated to the global economic situation and rather obeys a momentum effect and that most other virtual currencies are correlated during the first cryptocurrency. But this is less and less true and challengers manage to make remarkable breakthroughs like Tether or Litecoin for example. In addition to the macroeconomic context, upward factors linked to the evolutions of the cryptocurrency may exist as is for example the case of the Bitcoin halving, which takes place approximately every 4 years, the last having taken place on May 11. 2020.

 This phenomenon which consists, every 210,000 blocks of transactions, halving the reward for minors and almost systematically leads to an increase in prices.

RANKING OF VIRTUAL CURRENCIES ACCORDING TO THEIR 2021 STOCK MARKET VALUATION

You may be wondering which cryptocurrency to buy or looking for information on which cryptocurrency to invest in or which cryptocurrency to trade. Investors often favor cryptocurrencies with a substantial market capitalization and relatively high prices, which reflects certain confidence in the currency and relative strength of the token.

Discover the ranking of the 10 most important virtual currencies taking into account their market capitalization, that is to say, the total value of all tokens in circulation (the price of a token X number in circulation).

1. Bitcoin (BTC)

Creation date: 2009

Market capitalization as of January 7, 2021: $638.506 billion

Price variation over 1 year (USD): + 336% approximately

2. Ethereum (ETH)

Creation date: 2015

Market capitalization as of January 7, 2021: $129.635 billion

Price variation over 1 year (USD): approximately 725%

3. Tether (USDT)

Creation date: 2015

Market capitalization as of January 7, 2021: $22.181 billion

Price variation over 1 year (USD): - approximately 0.03%

4. Ripple (XRP)

Creation date: 2015

Market capitalization as of January 7, 2021: $11.399 billion

Price variation over 1 year (USD): around 18%

5. Litecoin (LTC)

Creation date: 2013

Market capitalization as of January 7, 2021: $10.218 billion

Price variation over 1 year (USD): approximately 267%

6. Cardano (ADA)

Date of creation: 2017

Market capitalization as of January 7, 2021: $9.102 billion

Price variation over 1 year (USD): approximately 705%

7. Polkadot (DOT)

Date of creation: 2020

Market capitalization January 7, 2021: $8.868 billion

Price variation over 1 year (USD): approximately 242%

8. Bitcoin Cash (BCH)

Creation date: 2017

Market capitalization January 7, 2021: $8.012 billion

Price variation over 1 year (USD): approximately 85%

9. Stellar (XLM)

Creation date: 2014

Market capitalization January 7, 2021: $6.658 billion

Price variation over 1 year (USD): approximately 539%

10. Chainlink (LINK)

Date of creation: 2017

Market capitalization January 7, 2021: $6.386 billion

Price variation over 1 year (USD): approximately 684%

WHAT IS CRYPTOCURRENCY USED FOR?

Virtual currency is a means of payment for the purchase of goods and services. What are the reasons for using cryptocurrency? Like any currency, cryptocurrencies allow the purchase of goods and services. Not being under the influence of a central authority and escaping any regulation, they have long been the preserve of illegal transactions (ransomware, drug trafficking, etc.) but they tend to shed their bad reputation by democratizing and attracting a wider audience. Today, cryptocurrencies are increasingly used for legal transactions.

Virtual currencies, like Bitcoin, allow the purchase of many common consumer goods. For example, it is possible to buy with Bitcoins, computer equipment of course, but also food, jewelry, decorative objects, cultural products, etc. Overstock, a general merchant site, accepts payment in Bitcoins, just like Shopify.

Paying for everyday goods with other cryptocurrencies is more difficult, but not impossible. The Ether, for example, could be used to buy works of art exhibited by young artists at La Compagnie (Paris X) in the spring of 2017. The virtual currency which wants to compete with Bitcoin has thus done, on this occasion, its entry into the real world. At the end of 2021, Paypal said in a statement its intention to "join the cryptocurrency market [...] by allowing customers to buy, sell and hold bitcoin and other digital assets, using the company's online wallet accounts". This announcement allows considering certain and rapid democratization of virtual currencies that will be offered by this giant of online payment. Despite everything, it is more difficult today to carry out a transaction of everyday life in cryptocurrency than with the currency that is currently in the country where you live. Ditto for digital payments.

However, cryptocurrencies could eventually lower the cost of a digital transaction. And the financial and banking sector is watching these advances very closely. In the future, electronic payment based on cryptographic evidence may be the norm.

Enough to embarrass the banks by forcing them to completely review the transaction model!

Cryptocurrency as a financial asset for investing

Cryptocurrencies must find their balance between means of payment and financial assets. Because it is indeed good on which investors have positioned themselves en masse in recent years. For many people who have flocked to these new kinds of financial assets, cryptocurrencies are first and foremost a potentially profitable investment.

However, are virtual currencies an investment like any other? What is certain is that digital alternative currencies can constitute a new kind of investment, while participating in the new digital economy. It is common to include crypto-currencies in the category of various goods and other atypical investments. This typology is relevant in the sense that it calls for prudence and to invest only a whole part of its capital in such assets.

Bitcoin was around $20,000 in December 2017 after a

record year when the famous cryptocurrency saw its price multiplied by 15 in dollars. And Bitcoin has been in the news again recently with a spectacular rise in late 2020 that continues into early 2021 with a high of over $40,000 reached on January 7. Even if these dazzling price increases are accompanied by consequent volatility, we understand the interest that can arouse the virtual currencies, able to display impressive performances which are matched only by their volatility. The increase in the volume of trade and the massive rise in the market capitalization of virtual currencies clearly indicates the interest of investors in these new financial assets.

Keep in mind, however, that buying cryptocurrencies more or less amounts to betting on innovative technology. If the digital currency you have invested in becomes dominant (they all try with varying degrees of success to dethrone Bitcoin), you will have made a good deal. Ethereum remains the great challenger of Bitcoin with a market capitalization close to the most famous of the cryptocurrencies.

Note also that online brokers are starting to offer trading in crypto-currencies like Bitcoin, notably via CFDs.

The Intercontinental Exchange (ICE), the parent company of the New York Stock Exchange (NYSE), the New York Stock Exchange, is at the origin of the "Bakkt" platform, specializing in Bitcoin and crypto-currencies, which allows 'buy, sell, spend and even store Bitcoins. Its Bitcoin futures are listed on a federally regulated market. An initiative that clearly reflects the interest of major financial players in cryptocurrencies.

Some do not even hesitate to compare crypto-currencies to gold, considering that in both cases, it is a safe haven. We can even go so far as to think that Bitcoin and other cryptocurrencies are the digital gold of young generations who do not maintain the same relationship as the previous ones with the precious yellow metal.

Crypto-equity crowdfunding: another use of cryptocurrency

Finally, crypto-currencies have another function, more niche but just as important: the financing of projects by raising funds from people (individuals and institutional investors or business angels).

You may be wondering: what is a cryptocurrency ICO? It is neither more nor less than fundraising in cryptocurrency. Crypto-currencies can indeed also be used to finance companies via crypto-equity crowdfunding, crowdfunding in virtual currencies. The process, which has developed significantly since 2014, consists of financing equity crowdfunding through virtual currency. This type of practice is referred to by the term ICO or Initial Coin Offering. Several platforms offer this solution, such as Swarm for example.

WHAT MAKES THE VALUE OF A CRYPTOCURRENCY?

Why is a cryptocurrency going down? Why is a cryptocurrency falling? How does a cryptocurrency increase in value? Find out what are the factors that influence crypto prices.

CONFIDENCE IN VIRTUAL CURRENCY

First, as with any currency, virtual or real, the founding element is trust. People need to trust cryptocurrencies in general and trust a particular cryptocurrency, but that's not impossible - far from it. During the Greek crisis, some massively bought Bitcoin, a currency that inspired them more confidence than that, real and regulated, which suffered the full brunt of the monetary crisis and had to face galloping inflation.

The number of users of the cryptocurrency

What also makes the value of a virtual currency is the importance of its network and the number of people who use it all over the world.

The more users a cryptocurrency has, the more its value increases, which means that the price of the token goes up. Two essential factors will push people to buy a virtual currency: the penetration rate in the real economy (i.e. the ease with which one can buy goods and services in real life by paying with said cryptocurrency) and the prospect of

positioning itself in a crypto-asset while achieving a relatively large capital gain.

Speculation is still the main driver of the development of cryptocurrencies and their prices vary considerably depending on the appreciation of traders who think they will make money easily or not on a particular token, creating bubbles as in 2017-2018. Intrinsic value doesn't

really come into play. And the situation is very likely to continue as long as demand in the real economy remains relatively weak.

The growing democratization of virtual currencies is boosting the price of cryptos

The democratization of virtual currencies reflects the growing confidence of the general public in this type of asset. Individuals will now be able to pay for more purchases of goods and services via virtual currencies with their Paypal account as we have seen previously or with the future Facebook token, the Diem, which will make it possible to pay for purchases on the marketplace of the famous social network.

Governments and central banks are also showing more inclination to adopt virtual currencies with an effort made on the regulation of cryptocurrencies and the emergence of digital currencies from central banks. Finally, the financial markets also seem to be making room for cryptos. Many brokers now offer to invest in virtual currencies. Several large investment banks have a unit dedicated to crypto assets, and more and more traditional funds and hedge funds are positioning themselves in crypto assets. Last notable event: Coinbase, the American cryptocurrency exchange platform, should soon go public.

HOW TO INVEST IN CRYPTOCURRENCY?

One in four people has already bought cryptocurrency. One in three people intends to buy them according to the February 2018 study carried out by the Paypite Association. If 94% of people over 60 do not intend to buy, according to the same study, a poll for "Les

Echos" by Odoxa-Linxea in January 2018 indicated that a quarter of 18-24-year-olds are considering buying them, and 36% of them even think that they will one day replace the official currencies. According to a study carried out in April 2019 by the crypto exchange BitFlyer, two-thirds of 10,000 Europeans surveyed believe that cryptocurrencies will still be there in ten years. However, barely a tenth of that surveyed bet on the use of cryptos as a currency in the future.

The Paypite study also reveals that 18% of French people do not know how to buy cryptocurrency. If you are not lacking the desire but do not know how to proceed, find here our explanations and advice for positioning yourself in cryptocurrency.

2 ways to buy your virtual currency

There are two ways to get cryptocurrencies:

- by selling a good or a service and demanding payment in the cryptocurrency of your choice;

- by converting "classic" currencies (euro, dollar, etc.) into encrypted currency.

Kraken, Bitstamp, Poloniex, Coinbase, or even Circle make it possible, for example, to convert euros into Bitcoins quite easily, or even into other virtual currencies.

To convert your euros into Bitcoins, you must register on this platform by providing an electronic copy of an identity document and a recent invoice (gas, electricity, internet) to prove your address.

CHOOSE YOUR CRYPTOCURRENCY EXCHANGE PLATFORM OR VIRTUAL CURRENCY BROKER

To avoid scams and see more clearly in the offer of crypto-currency intermediaries, the Pacte law has set up a new specific regime governing these service providers on digital assets (PSAN). According to the AMF, these PSANs bring together all the "financial intermediaries who offer various services relating to an investment in crypto-assets". Since December 2020, these PSANs must, in order to be able to offer crypto-asset custody services or access to crypto-assets or the purchase/sale of crypto-assets against currencies having legal tender, must be registered with the financial market policeman who will ensure the reliability of the service provider. Any player who has not registered may find himself on the AMF's blacklists. In addition, an optional authorization can also be requested by the PSAN which, after having obtained it, will have the right to be able to canvass new customers.

Before any investment and any transaction, check that the actor with whom you plan to deal is not on the AMF blacklists, that he is registered with the Autorité des Marchés Financiers and, if you are canvassed, that this actor has the authorization which gives him the right to do so. Note that it is also possible to trade cryptocurrencies through derivatives offered by online brokers.

Create a cryptocurrency wallet

Whatever your method of obtaining, you will have to create a "wallet" in order to keep your change.

A crypto wallet is an address in the form of a series of numbers that can be accessed by means of a password.

You can create a Bitcoin address and password for yourself for free and quite simply on a dedicated platform like BitAddress.org for example. For other crypto-currencies, other specific platforms exist. Cryptoryptanor thus supports several currencies.

Finally, to pay with a cryptocurrency (or receive a payment in cryptocurrency), an intermediary is necessary. You will have the choice between:

- an exchange platform similar to a broker;
- software to download.

Please note, these intermediaries usually charge commissions. We also cannot recommend enough that you choose your intermediary carefully, many of them have already gone bankrupt.

Also, watch out for scams of all kinds that flourish on the web and "brokers" who refuse to return the sums held in your account.

HOW TO TRADE CRYPTOCURRENCY?

All over the world, new initiatives are developing to invest in the cryptocurrency market. Thus, as we have seen, the New York Stock Exchange announced in August 2018 the creation of the "Bakkt" platform by the Intercontinental Exchange (ICE), the parent company of the New York Stock Exchange (NYSE), which allows you to buy, sell and store Bitcoins. But the United States is also seeing the creation of trust companies specializing in cryptocurrencies such as LLC and ITbit, two companies which, in addition to meeting the requirements of the New York State Department in terms of capitalization, reserves, compliance, protection of consumers, and cybersecurity, also provide guarantees of computer storage systems and cold storage vault systems for Bitcoin holdings of the famous GABI fund.

The individual who wants to position himself on the crypto-currency market can turn to a specialized online broker who offers virtual currency trading via CFDs.

For example, eToro allows you to trade Bitcoin, Ethereum, Ripple, Bitcoin Cash, and Cardano.

IG allows you to trade Bitcoin, Ethereum, Ripple, and Litecoin. You will also be limited in terms of leverage. Indeed, a CFD on crypto-actives cannot have leverage greater than two. Recall that 89.4% of retail traders lose money according to the Study of results of retail investors on CFDs and Forex trading in France carried out by the Autorité des Marchés Financiers on the basis of the results obtained by nearly 15,000 French retail traders from 2009 to 2013. The AMF also points out that the financial intermediary who markets this type of CFD must be approved.

CRYPTOCURRENCY TAXATION 2021: HOW TO CALCULATE THE CAPITAL GAIN AND DECLARE THE GAINS IN VIRTUAL CURRENCY

Capital gains generated by the activity of buying and reselling cryptocurrencies are taxable as "digital assets" since 1 st January 2019. This is the flat tax of 30% which applies to gains from cryptocurrency trading activities. The taxpayer nevertheless has a transfer allowance of 305 euros per year.

Note: transactions are only taxable when converting virtual currencies into traditional currencies such as the euro, the dollar, or the Swiss franc, including if the money remains on the exchange platform without moving.

The number of its capital gains must be indicated in the income tax return, in the box "Capital gains or losses on digital assets", to which must be attached the form 2086 providing details of taxable transactions.

6 TIPS FOR INVESTING IN CRYPTOCURRENCY

1. Understanding Blockchain Technology

Before investing in this type of currency, make sure that you understand this innovation and especially the technology behind it. This ultimately comes down to fully studying the Blockchain technology from which cryptocurrencies originate. Also, and especially, pay attention to the details that differentiate currencies from one another: the programming language, the blockchain validation system, governance, the currency's ability to adapt to an order of magnitude change of demand for example.

2. Take into consideration the token expansion limit

The unit of cryptocurrency is called a token. The number of tokens created can be limited, as is the case with Bitcoin which will be limited to 21 million Bitcoins in circulation, making the product relatively rare, which of course contributes to its value. But a cryptocurrency can also follow a deflationary pattern. In this case, the quantity of

money in circulation is unlimited, which could over time encourage the stagnation (or even the decrease) of its price.

3. Check the transparency of virtual currency

Favor a cryptocurrency with a website with clearly identified investors and developers, a presentation of the project, possibly a roadmap indicating the planned technological advances. If none of this is accessible, beware, you could invest in a Ponzi scheme.

4. Stay informed on cryptocurrency websites

To be up to date in this ultra-niche and ultra-geek field, and therefore ensure an investment under the best conditions by having all the information on the targeted asset, it is better to look for the information where it is found, that is to say on the web! Many cryptocurrencies offer their own websites but broaden your search to community websites like Reddit or Slack which will allow you to publish, consult sections, discuss and share issues and opinions. The Bitcoin talk forum fulfills the same role but is exclusively devoted to cryptocurrencies (not just Bitcoin because it has a dedicated altcoin section).

5. Learn about the quality of virtual currency developers and their funding

What makes the success of a cryptocurrency above all is the quality of the developers who are at the origin of this innovation. So check their experience, education, work history, etc. Do they form a tight-knit team with good rapport? You can verify that their interactions on the Slack or Reddit community are both cordial and constructive.

Finally, you must know who pays the developers: a company or a private equity fund outside of cryptocurrency? Are developers paid with their cryptocurrency? The important thing is to be able to assess the motivation of developers and any conflicts of interest.

6. Limit your investments in these volatile high-risk assets

Volatility is one of the major characteristics of cryptocurrencies. Thus, the value of a cryptocurrency, i.e. its price, can increase or decrease, very quickly, in an unpredictable way. In the question: its young economy, its unusual nature, and especially its sometimes-illiquid markets.

And the number of platforms further adds to the lack of liquidity of the tokens. Thus, at the end of 2019, "a volume of 143 bitcoins is enough to vary its price by 1% on the Bitstamp platform. Coinbase and Kraken are much more liquid, and it is respectively 456 and 672 bitcoins that must be exchanged to move the price of the leader in cryptos by 1%" reports the site Les Echos.

Investing in cryptocurrency is therefore not recommended for cautious profiles with a strong aversion to risk. For others, think all the same not to keep a large part of your

savings in Bitcoin or others which remain high-risk assets. There is a real risk of losing a large part of the money invested in this way.

If the cryptocurrency adventure tempts you, go for it with money that you are ready to lose. It must be an investment representing a very small part of your financial assets. Cryptocurrency is more of an experiment to try if you feel like it than a reasoned investment made with a view to diversification. Wanting to make money really fast is never a good reason to invest in cryptocurrency.

The Principles of Cryptocurrency

As the name suggests, cryptocurrency, also known as Bitcoins and Litecoin among others, is crypto and virtual currency. But then, why use a virtual currency when you have access to your bank account via the Internet? Indeed, you can make transfers, online payments ... Anonymity is the first reason for the emergence of such a currency. It is indeed possible to pay for purchases in complete anonymity. Very interesting to avoid any risk of hacking on your current bank account. In addition, and this is where some will find cryptocurrency interesting, it escapes any banking system already in place. This means that nothing controls it and no one controls it enough to regulate it.

Where to Use Such A Currency? At What Cost?

Every day, the list of websites and merchants allowing Bitcoin purchases is growing. Thus, you can easily buy leather goods, beauty products, computer equipment, video games, and even services. Bitcoins are invading online payment. Its asset? It does not depend on any regulatory authority or any banking entity. You can therefore pay, be paid, make payments to a third party, even international, without paying any fees. A reality that is becoming more than attractive in the eyes of many merchants who today have to pay a percentage of their turnover to banks for each transaction made with a bank card.

A Real Alternative System Shaking Up the Banking World

Obviously, such a system arouses the suspicions or curiosity of professionals in the banking system. It would not be about seeing a complex and profitable system swept away by a cryptocurrency.

The whole world of finance would be shaken. This is why many are studying this currency which, on paper, has only advantages. But now, who says "anonymity" and "deregulation" also says "money laundering", "organized crime", "parallel markets".

That's the concern if no transaction is traceable, how can you be sure that you are not laundering money, that you are not buying illegal products? This is the crux of the matter.

Advantages of Cryptocurrencies

- They are global currencies

These virtual currencies are not regulated by any type of governmental organization, such as the State, banks, financial institutions, or companies. This gives the possibility of being able to use them anywhere in the world.

For example, Bitcoin claims that "in the same way that no one controls the technology behind email, Bitcoin also has no owners." Thus, this type of cryptocurrency is controlled by all its users. Therefore, although programmers improve their software, they cannot make a change without the consent of all customers.

- They are safe

According to experts, counterfeiting or duplication of cryptocurrencies is impossible thanks to a sophisticated combination of proven cryptographic techniques. In this sense, each person has cryptographic keys that are necessary to carry out any type of digital operation.

- Some cryptocurrencies are deflationary

Cryptocurrencies such as Bitcoin or Litecoin have limited the issuance of their virtual currencies. In the case of Bitcoin, at 21 million and Litecoin at 84 million. This turns them into deflationary cryptocurrencies, as the issuance of these digital currencies reduces over time.

- They have irreversible transactions

Another of its advantages are irreversible transactions. That is, if cryptocurrencies are used, no third party can cancel or modify a transaction already carried out. This is so because they are not regulated by a central body that can access them.

- They are characterized by their immediacy

One of their advantages in e-commerce, for example, is its immediacy. If we have international clients, this payment method could greatly speed up the exchange process, especially between banks in countries that do not have agreements with each other and have to go through a central bank, causing payment processes to be delayed several days.

- They are transparent

All transactions made through the Blockchain are public. The blockchain file is stored on multiple computers on a network, and not in one place. Thus, this type of storage allows it to be readable for all users, making it transparent and difficult to alter.

Disadvantages of Cryptocurrencies

At the same time, we find a series of disadvantages in cryptocurrencies that may be the cause of their non-establishment in society and their mistrust in potential and future users.

- Possible loss of money

One of its main dangers, and its most risky characteristic, is that if you lose the private key to access your wallet, you lose all the money you had in it since it is virtual money. Therefore, it is advisable to have a backup of your wallet to avoid this fatal situation.

- Changes and lack of regulation

Currently, work is being done on its regulation and there are several directives of the European Union pending approval.

In Spain, given the vertiginous expansion that cryptocurrencies have been having, in particular for the use of remittances and also as an investment asset, new regulations on the matter are expected. In this sense, the State Agency for the Tax Directorate of Spain points out that "in relation to the fiscal risks observed in operations carried out with cryptocurrencies", actions will continue based on the general guidelines contained in the Tax and Customs Control Plan.

- Mistrust in potential users

Although the trend of cryptocurrencies has been growing in recent years, many companies have not yet dared to use this virtual currency. One, due to the risk of price fluctuations, and two, due to the ignorance of the benefits that cryptocurrencies can bring.

Chapter 2
History of Bitcoin

itcoin is the oldest and best-known cryptocurrency in the world. The history of Bitcoin is very colorful and includes several exciting events. History helps understand the present, and knowing the history of Bitcoin is recommended to anyone interested in Bitcoin and other cryptocurrencies. The aim of this text is to introduce Bitcoin and its history.

Bitcoin's story officially began in 2008 when an unknown person or organization using the nickname Satoshi Nakamoto was looking for programmers to help him on a Bitcoin project. However, Satoshi is said to have developed Bitcoin longer. Satoshi Nakamoto's goal was to create a fully decentralized, virtual payment system that uses a revolutionary technology called a blockchain.

Nakamoto created Bitcoin completely independently of third parties such as governments, central banks, and various institutions. Bitcoin's official website was registered in August 2008. In October 2008, Satoshi Nakamoto published Bitcoin's whitepaper, in which he described the operations and the technology behind them to Bitcoin employees. The first Bitcoin block, better known as the Genesis Block, was mined on January 3, 2009. The day the Bitcoin Block was created is now commonly viewed as the Bitcoin Birthday. The first Bitcoin transaction was made on January 12th, 2009 between Satoshi Nakamoto and software developer Hal Finney. Satoshi Nakamoto has mined for most of the earliest blocks on the Bitcoin blockchain. He collected a pot with more than a million bitcoins for himself. At that time, the level of difficulty in mining was low and it was possible to mine new bitcoins very quickly.

The early 2010s

Satoshi Nakamoto created Bitcoin at the best possible time. In 2008 and 2009 the world was hit by an unprecedented financial crisis. This economic crisis was the result of the reckless monetary policy of the central banks. Confidence in traditional banks had collapsed and people were waiting for a new type of monetary system. In the first half of the 2010s, Bitcoin's popularity began to grow tremendously, and it was also possible to use Bitcoin to shop in the real world for the first time. The first real-world purchase was made with bitcoins on May 22, 2010, when a person named Laszlo Hanyez bought two pizzas with 10,000 bitcoins. This day is now known as Bitcoin Pizza Day. In 2010, numerous new services around Bitcoin began to develop. The best known of these services was the Bitcoin exchange called Mt. Gox. The story of the mountain. Gox ended in 2014 after massive hacker attacks. Mt. Gox's hacking remains one of the most dramatic events in Bitcoin history to date. The last sign of Bitcoin founder Satoshi Nakamoto was in 2011 when he said in an email that he would move on to other things.

Satoshi transferred responsibility for the project to a programmer named Gavin Andersen, who also became the lead developer of the Bitcoin Foundation. In 2011, the the world saw the first bitcoin price bubble when the price of bitcoin rose from less than a dollar to $30 and then returned to $2.

Years of Bitcoin Growth

Bitcoin's popularity has grown tremendously since its early years. Bitcoin's use cases have increased, and more and more investors around the world have recognized the potential of Bitcoin as an investment. Bitcoin has seen three price bubbles in the course of its history. One of these occurred in late 2013 when the price of Bitcoin rose from a hundred dollars to over $1,000 in just a few months. After that, the price of bitcoin was on a downward trend until January 2015, when the price of one bitcoin was less than $200. However, interest in bitcoin and blockchain technology increased. In 2016, Bitcoin established itself as a phenomenon that could not go unnoticed by banks. Interest in Bitcoin exploded and this was also reflected in the price of Bitcoin. The price of Bitcoin rose steadily from the beginning of 2015 to 2017. In late 2017, Bitcoin experienced the third price bubble in its history, when the price of Bitcoin rose to nearly $20,000. As expected, the sharp rise in prices also led to an increase in media interest.

At the turn of the year 2017 and 2018, the interest in Bitcoin was greater than ever before. The sharp rise in the value of Bitcoin also led to a tightening of Bitcoin regulation. The regulation of Bitcoin has been tightened, e.g. B. in China and South Korea. Bitcoin has had different forks throughout its history received, d. H. Upgrades. One of Bitcoin's most famous forks was in 2017 when Bitcoin's SegWit update was carried out. The SegWit update improved the capacity of the Bitcoin network by changing the way the network secures Bitcoin transactions. The time before the SegWit update was also controversial in the Bitcoin community. The bitcoin community has been divided into two different groups. Another group wanted to improve the capacity of the Bitcoin network by increasing the block size of the blockchain. In contrast, the other party wanted to improve Bitcoin's scalability through Lightning network technology. In practice, lightning network technology means that smaller Bitcoin transactions are transmitted on a completely separate network. Eventually, the controversy about Bitcoin's scalability escalated to the point that a group demanding larger block sizes pulled out of the Bitcoin community as its own cryptocurrency before the SegWit update went into effect. This cryptocurrency is known today as Bitcoin Cash. The increasing interest in Bitcoin led to an accelerated exchange of new cryptocurrencies and the introduction of more Bitcoin-related investment products like options and certificates in the 2010s. At the same time, Bitcoin has become part of a portfolio of more and more private investors and institutions. The growing popularity of Bitcoin and other cryptocurrencies has also led to an increase in market regulation for cryptocurrencies in recent years.

Bitcoin was the world's first digital currency and was introduced over a decade ago. Even though Bitcoin eventually did the pioneering work, there were also attempts to introduce digital currencies before that.

Satoshi Nakamoto, the person or group behind Bitcoin (the exact identity is still unknown), mined the first Bitcoin block called "Genesis". The next big event happened in

2010 when Laszlo Hanyecz paid for two pizzas with BTC. For the first time, BTC was used to purchase physical goods in the real world.

IPO

In the same year, the first exchanges for cryptocurrencies were launched. In 2013, over ten different cryptocurrencies could already be traded. Thousands of cryptocurrencies have been created in the past few years and the market has grown steadily since then. As the world of cryptocurrencies continues to expand and grow in popularity, they are being accepted as a means of payment by more and more shops, brands, and networks around the world.

With the growing popularity and use of these digital currencies, the value of Cryptocurrencies and with it the amount of trading profits has increased.

Trading Software

Trading software for trading digital assets such as Bitcoin Era makes it easier for people with no trading experience to buy and sell digital currencies and benefit from these trades.

Bitcoin Era

Bitcoin Era is a trading system that can be used to trade cryptocurrencies manually or automatically. The manual and automated modes that the software offers make profitable trading in Bitcoin and other cryptocurrencies a breeze for everyone.

Trade Bots

Today, many teams offer paid and free crypto trading bots for Bitcoin and other cryptocurrencies. Learn More About Trading Bot: Trading Bots could be used to effortlessly automate the complicated and seemingly impossible strategies of the cleverest traders.

Why Was Bitcoin Created?

Bitcoin was created in 2009 following the writing of a white paper entitled "A Peer-to-Peer Electronic Payment

System" written by one or more people appearing under the pseudonym Satoshi Nakamoto. So why did you create Bitcoin?

There are 3 main reasons for the creation of Bitcoin: the development of e-commerce, the loss of confidence in financial institutions, and the resolution of the problem of double value. The development of e-commerce is generating exponential growth in international financial exchanges. Carried out by banks, these processes are often long and expensive in transaction costs. These transaction costs remunerate the bank which will insure any disputes between the buyer and the seller. These fees could also compensate for the phenomena of fraud which are considered inevitable by the banks. All these reasons have led banks to offer a system of reversibility of payments in the event of error, fraud or even default by the seller or the buyer.

Bitcoin, by introducing a cryptographic transaction verification system, eliminates the need for a trusted third party. Transactions are carried out directly from user A to user B, almost instantaneously and without generating transaction fees.

In addition, Bitcoin was created so that you no longer have to place your trust in banks to carry out transactions.

Transactions are validated cryptographically. In other words, sellers will no longer have to worry about buyers defaulting on payment.

Finally, the creation of Bitcoin is also a response to a technical problem encountered by the first attempt at digital currency called "B-money". This problem is that of a double value. It is okay to send a copy of an attachment by email; however, it becomes a huge problem when you want to send money! Impossible to send 1 euro while keeping 1 euro! Bitcoin responds technically to this problem by introducing blockchain technology which keeps a precise record of all the transactions carried out on the network. Thus, all users know the owners of Bitcoins at all times!

Chapter 3
Bitcoin Investment Process

I n the heat of bitcoin, brokers and exchange houses have proliferated that offer to buy virtual currency. These are some of the most time-consuming and can be classified as secure pages to acquire bitcoins and other cryptocurrencies:

- Coinbase: it is one of the largest websites and also one of the best known. Its advantage is that it is easy to use and very intuitive. The negative part is the commissions that you charge when making any transaction (3.5%). Allows payment by card and transfer.

- Kraken: It is cheaper than Coinbase and also one of the largest. Its commission does not reach 0.3% for the purchase of bitcoins and also allows free transfers in Europe.

- Bitstamp: another of the largest houses in which the commissions are linked to the volume of the operation.
- Cex.io - They accept euros, pounds, dollars, rubles, and even Ethereum to buy bitcoins.
- LocalBitcoins: unlike the rest, this platform has specialized in P2P buying, that is, between users. It does not charge a commission, but it is more complicated to manage than the larger houses.

How to save your bitcoins?

In the world of cryptocurrencies, investment is one thing and storage is another. As in plans and funds, there is a manager and a depository entity, in that of bitcoins, there are bitcoins wallets. Most houses are responsible for saving the bitcoins in which you invest for you eliminating this problem.

In addition, most also operate as a wallet for those bitcoins, so you do not have to physically save them on your computer. This involves the risk of leaving the security of your investment in the hands of others, but it also eliminates the risk that you could lose those bitcoins or that they will be stolen.

1. All platforms will ask you to verify your identity with your ID and other proofs. So that? They do this to avoid money laundering. Most of the movements with cryptocurrencies are very difficult to trace (hence the word "crypto") and verifying the identity of buyers and sellers prevents this type of crime.
2. Investments in cryptocurrencies are VERY volatile.
3. Due to the high risk of this type of investment, DO NOT invest an amount of money that you are not willing to lose.

Best cryptocurrencies to invest in 2021

What have been the most profitable cryptocurrencies of 2020 and so far in 2021? What currencies have achieved the best returns? The following list includes the ones that accrue the most benefits for a year.

- Ave. Accumulates profitability of + 6398.22% in the last year.
- Kusama. Accumulates profitability of + 5222.37% in the last year.
- Celsius Network. It accumulated profitability of +3,843.88% in the last year.
- Band Protocol. Accumulated profitability of +2850.66% in the last year.
- Theta Token. Accumulated profitability of +2299.39% in the last year.
- Reserve Rights. Accumulated profitability of +2,138.28% in the last year.
- Loopring. Accumulated profitability of +1939.66% in the last year.
- THORChain. Accumulated profitability of +1797.66% in the last year.

- SwissBorg. Accumulated profitability of +1669.58% in the last year
- Zilliga. Accumulated profitability of +1454.44% in the last year.

In addition, in this very complex year, the technology sector is one of the most boosted. All this situation has caused online sales to skyrocket, the use of food delivery platforms at home, to watch series and movies, etc. This has caused the big technology companies to have had a strong rebound in the stock market, placing the RV Technology Sector category among the best performing so far this year. For this reason, at Finect we have developed this showcase with the best funds that invest in technology companies at the moment:

Most profitable cryptocurrencies

As the stock market saying goes, past returns do not ensure future returns. The evolution of a virtual currency is a good indication of its potential, but that does not mean that it is the best cryptocurrency to invest in in 2021. The price of virtual currencies, with falls of over 50% on many occasions, is a good example. Is this an indication that you have to flee the sector in a hurry? Not much less, just that the price was too inflated.

What cryptocurrencies are performing best in 2021? This is a list of digital currencies with the best future taking into account their potential and evolution so far.

Bitcoin

Whether we like it or not, bitcoin is still the main cryptocurrency, and the best to invest, which sets the standard for the behavior of the rest of virtual currencies. There are several reasons why investing in bitcoin can be thought of as a reasonable investment, and it is because it is decentralized, that is, there is no central institution that controls the supply of bitcoin.

Ethereum

Ehtereum is a great alternative to Bitcoin and the second virtual currency in terms of capitalization. Still far from the leader and discarded the possibility of it surpassing it as digital money, its strength is in the development of applications and how it uses smart contracts in development environments.

Ethereum and Ether were already some of the most profitable cryptocurrencies in years past.

An alternative to direct investment in Ethereum is to buy cryptocurrencies based on technology such as Aragon or Stox.

Ripple

Ripple is another of the largest currencies in terms of capitalization after Bitcoin, Ethereum, or Bitcoin Cash. It is a currency that has grown less than the rest in the last quarter of last year and that has great potential.

Ripple is not a rookie, since it has 5 years of life. It is based on technology and allows up to 1,000 transactions per second, much faster than Bitcoin. In addition, its technology can be used as a protocol

IOTA

IOTA is one of the most ambitious projects in the cryptocurrency arena. Its objective is to incorporate virtual currencies into the internet of things and it does so by neglecting the blockchain the technology used by most currencies of this type. IOTA is based on Tangle technology, which in theory is much more scalable, faster, and lighter than blockchain.

NEO

Known as China's Ethereum, its future will be linked to what the Asian giant decides about the future of cryptocurrencies. The Chinese government has already announced greater control over the sector.

Litecoin

Litecoin is one of the veterans in the sector. Created in 2011, it sought to reduce transaction time compared to bitcoin.

Like Bitcoin, Litecoin's limit is 84 million coins of which there are already about 55 million in circulation.

Reddcoin

Reddcoin or RDD is one of the low-cost cryptocurrencies. It defines itself as a trending currency and its use is limited to social networks.

Reddcoin has its own social tipping platform that can now be used on Twitter and Reddit.

Monero

Monero is an anonymous cryptocurrency. With it, the details of the coin transaction cannot be traced. That is its main strength compared to other options and what gives it value.

Chapter 4
Cryptocurrency Market

Cryptocurrencies are born from new technologies. They are born *from the technology called "Blockchain" or blocks.* It is a type of programming that will allow what is done to be seen by everyone. And it is here, right here at this point, that gives security to cryptocurrencies.

Who produces the cryptocurrencies? They are produced by miners, who are usually programmers who have very powerful computer equipment, with the requirements that are demanded to generate this "blockchain" technology. When a new cryptocurrency is produced, what happens is that the entire community sees it, because the connection that exists in the computers prevents one of them from erasing the trace that has been

119

left on the internet of the creation of that cryptocurrency.

So, what are cryptocurrencies? They are virtual currencies that we are going to use as a means of payment or also to receive money. This is what makes the receptions and payments that are made, are made without financial intermediaries.

Therefore, it is a currency that *does not have state control.* There is no central bank of a country or a central bank of a community, such as the European Economic Community, that can say something for or against what cryptocurrencies are. Therefore, they do not have legal control.

This has its benefits and it obviously has its drawbacks as well. The inconvenient part is that the person does not feel very safe, because maybe if he does not know much about what blockchain technology is, he could be quite afraid to put his money in a private company that is offering you a number that will be the one that will identify your cryptocurrency.

They are a quick correction of letters and numbers that make you the owner of that virtual currency. So, what are they? They are virtual currencies that serve us both to receive money and to pay with them and that of course, being quoted in a market, cause that due to the effect of buying and selling, sometimes they go up more, other times they go down more because one can buy or sell them and this will therefore produce a fluctuation between that cryptocurrency and its exchange, either **with another cryptocurrency or with a legal tender**.

Let us remember that dollar or euro-type legal tender coins

are currencies that are also crossing with cryptocurrencies and that is where they intend to make a profit.

Well, I would say that we have to make cryptocurrencies simply for a very easy reason because they have come to stay and as more countries accept them and to the extent, especially that large companies such as Amazon start, for example, to admitting them as a form of payment will be highly complicated for cryptocurrencies not to stay with us.

For how much that blockchain technology has changed the way of seeing the risks. What I have commented on before, does not have control right now, there is no state or a central bank that is regulating them, but it is the trust of all the members of the blockchain system that allows cryptocurrencies to be considered more or less safe.

Of course, there have already been some cases in which, since it has been seen that at the beginning they gave problems but each time they are improving more and this is a positive point in their favor. How to do them? We have two possibilities.

That you organize yourself as a miner **if you are a computer programmer and you consider the possibility of producing them yourself**. With which it is obviously enough to have a payment for their services.

Or the other possibility would be that you buy them. To buy cryptocurrencies we would have to go to a house that sells them to us. It would have to be one of these private companies that are producers or have a large fund of cryptocurrencies. What cryptocurrencies to invest in? Well, we have several. Although there is one that takes the cake, which is called Bitcoin. *Bitcoin would be the first cryptocurrency*. They came out in 2008. At first, many people thought that well, it would not be something that would stay and would not really produce profits, that it would be a passing fad.

However, things changed with some people from Silicon Valley especially a highly known man like Bill Gates who began to take a lot of interest in them.

It was the year in which the cryptocurrency Bitcoin was more or less at about 200 two hundred and more dollars and it was at the entrance of the greats of Silicon Valley that made the cryptocurrency Bitcoin resurface and begin to rise. To give you an idea, since 2008 Bitcoin has reached $6,000, more or less its market ceiling.

Imagine the great fortunes that have been made for those people who bet on Bitcoin at the beginning. When it was in its origins, they cannot make a cryptocurrency and there are no other programmers who also consider the possibility of making cryptocurrencies again, different ones.

So **Ethereum also appeared,** which is currently trading in an environment of about three hundred-odd dollars.

We also have another cryptocurrency that would be Mitocoin or Litecoin is a cryptocurrency, perhaps it is one of the three that we can consider as best valued by the people who are the programmers and who are the ones who really understand its quality. The quality of a cryptocurrency goes a lot in the blockchain technology that is used to produce them. Hence, as technology advances, cryptocurrencies also become more powerful.

Here we have Bitcoin and now it has forked, it has made what is called a "fork". **What would a fork be?** Sorry, my English is not the best, but this word is written like this. Well, this is called a fork and Bitcoin has been forked mainly due to Bitcoin becoming highly expensive.

It is not in the capacity of everyone who really wants to acquire a single cryptocurrency like a Bitcoin and be paying it at 15 thousand and something dollars, which is what they are trading at right now.

So, what has been decided is to fork it and how it has been forked?

Generating Bitcoins of lower economic value, as would be the case of Bitcoin Cash or Bitcoin Gold, which would be the last two contributions to the technology that Bitcoin has. We will see if Bitcoin Cash or Bitcoin Gold end up staying and have effects similar to Bitcoin.

But notice that they are much smaller programmer communities. The next question that arises is ...

How do I buy it or where did you buy it?

Well, I can go buy it at the houses that produce and sell them. There are many companies like Coinbase like HABTC, and if like Bitfines or Bitstamp, perhaps, they say this is one of the best known, as it was a precursor when it came to producing Bitcoin.

Many people will say good and how do I do it? Well, to buy Bitcoin you usually have support in the house that sells them to you. It is the support that can help you in a guide when acquiring them, you have to generate what is called a wallet and in that wallet is where you will put your Bitcoin but I already advise you not to leave them within the internet network and to withdraw your cryptocurrency code out, that is, *on offline hardware.*

In this offline hardware what we are going to do is take your currency out of the servers. I know the case of some friends of mine who bought Bitcoin that in the beginning and that today having invested a figure like €500 or €1,000 at that time they would now have a small fortune. However, they had a problem, they did not save the password well and you are the only person who has access to that code. Without that code, you cannot re-enter, recover your Bitcoin, transfer it to another person or also exchange it for other currencies.

If you have not understood this 100%, if you have never invested in the stock market, if you have never approached a graph, I beg you, please do not make cryptocurrencies. Cryptocurrencies could be very dangerous for a layman. This is due to their wide fluctuations, to the very high volatility they have. It is required, if they are to be done in CFD's that you are already an expert trader and of course under no circumstances, buy them with the money you need for electricity, for the children's school, or to pay for your necessary issues.

Chapter 5
The concept of bitcoin mining

We are still exploring ways to invest and maximize cryptocurrencies such that you can make a profit, and mining is one of such investment pathways. Cryptocurrency mining appeals to investors because, as miners, they are rewarded for their work with crypto tokens. When you think about mining, see it as an entrepreneurial experience with cryptocurrencies with risks and rewards.

Crypto mining refers to how transactions between users are verified and added to the blockchain (public ledger). The mining process is responsible for the introduction of new coins into the crypto market, such that there is a constant supply of coins.

One of the essential features of cryptocurrencies is their decentralized peer-to-peer network, making it possible for the system to run without a significant third party.

But for this peer-to-peer process to work effectively, mining must be enabled, so miners are rewarded for the system progressive. Bitcoin is the most popular coin hence the reason it is the most "minable" coin as not all currencies can be mined. So how does this work?

As a miner, you get paid as an auditor because your role entails verifying legitimate bitcoin transactions. The process is meant to ensure that bitcoin users are honest, and it was founded by Bitcoin's creator Satoshi Nakamoto. Miners prevent the problem of double-spending and help bitcoin users gain increased trust in the system.

Double spending happens when the bitcoin owner spends the same bitcoin twice. This is not a problem with fiat because if you use a $5 bill to buy ice cream, you cannot use the same bill again.

But with digital currency, there is the potential risk where the owner could make another copy of the digital token and use it to transact with another party while holding on to its original.

However, a miner checks the transactions to ensure users do not try to spend the same bitcoin twice. After the miner verifies the bitcoin transaction, which is referred to as a "block," they are REWARDED with a quantity of bitcoin. But the reward is only gotten when the miner verifies up to 1MB (megabyte) worth of bitcoin transactions.

This realization means that not every miner earns the rewards because the Bitcoin creator set the mark at 1MB. There are two conditions to complete before a miner can earn the bitcoin;

- You must have verified 1MB worth of transactions.
- You must be the first one to get the right or closest answer to a numeric problem, and this process is called the "proof of work."

Mining pools

Sometimes two competing miners may broadcast a valid block simultaneously, and since only one can get the reward, they start to mine the set of blocks to ascertain who wins. The possibility of solving the problem is equal to the amount of total mining power of the network.

Therefore, miners with a small percentage of mining power have a limited chance of discovering their next block. To give such miners an advantage, mining pools are formed to make it easier for miners to pool their resources and share their processing power over one network. The miners then share the reward equally with everyone in the pool based on the amount of work they contribute to finding the block.

How much does a bitcoin miner earn?

When bitcoin was mined for the first time in 2009, the miner was paid 50 BTC for successfully mining bitcoin. In 2012, this reward was divided by two such that miners that year earned 25 BTC, and in 2016, the amount was divided by two again, making it 12.5 BTC. In May 2020, the reward was 6.25 BTC.

In November 2020, Bitcoin surged in price to one Bitcoin worth $17,900, so that means you may have earned up to $111,875 if you mined in May 2020. As the value of Bitcoin increases, miners will continually earn more even if the rewards reduce because now Bitcoin has risen to $50,000, now think of how much you will make if you were a miner.

How to become a bitcoin miner

Step one

Get bitcoin mining hardware.

It would help if you got a mining rig to get started, as this is the special hardware used for mining bitcoins or other cryptocurrencies. The rig is called Application-Specific Integrated Circuit Chips (ASIC), which mines bitcoin faster, uses less energy, is very powerful, and very expensive.

Before buying the rig, please consider these factors:

- The price (compare prices)
- Its hash performance rates and attempts at solving a block
- Its electric power consumption

Reading different miners' reviews will be helpful before choosing based on performance over price.

Please note that it is difficult to get this rig because of the high demand.

You can also check the ASIC WEB PAGE for detailed information about new miners before making a purchase.

Step two

Get your Bitcoin wallet.

Next, you need to set up a bitcoin wallet to receive your bitcoins and manage your addresses. As a beginner miner, you should use a software wallet because it is easy to operate, easily downloaded, and safe.

You can also a full version wallet like BITCOIN CORE which helps you decide on the blockchain that contains legitimate transactions.

Figure: Bitcoin Core image derived from *Master Data in Motion*

Step three

Join a mining pool

Even if you have the best mining hardware, you would still need to join a pool because that single hardware cannot compete in isolation with other miners around the world. When you enter a pool, the probability of solving the numeric problem and mining faster is higher, and then you share the rewards with others in the pool.

You can find different bitcoin mining pools for beginners, and if you are unsure of the one to join, please visit BITCOIN WIKI for credible pools. After selecting a pool, register on the website set your account, and wait for your "worker ID."

Step four

Get a mining program.

After getting the hardware, bitcoin wallet, and joined a mining pool, you will have to obtain a mining client for your computer. The mining client (mining software) connects you to the blockchain and bitcoin network while also delivering works to miners and collects the complete result of their jobs. The full information is then added to the blockchain.

There are many free mining programs for mining bitcoin, and some mining pools have their software. Before using any software, please read up on their advantages and disadvantages.

Step five

You can mine now!

Now you are ready to mine bitcoins. Connect your miner hardware to a power outlet, connect it with the computer and install the software. Fill in all information about your wallet and the mining pool you joined, then choose a device and start mining.

To become a successful miner, you must stay updated on crypto news because things change in the market suddenly, and you need always to know what's happening.

There are several ways of getting additional bitcoins, and mining is one such process that serves to keep the bitcoin system active while rewarding miners. This chapter provided all the information you need to understand how mining works, the gains, and how to get started.

Remember that as a practical guide, you are expected to follow through with the steps and approaches shared in this book. From the mining world, we will move on to the last chapter in this book that considers the future of Bitcoin.

Chapter 6
The future of Bitcoin

With all we have learned thus far, you will surely be curious about the future of bitcoin. You may be wondering if it will still be relevant in the future and make a worthwhile investment today that will be valuable in the future. In this last chapter, we will consider some predictions by experts in the cryptocurrency sector on what could happen in the future.

As mentioned throughout this material, cryptocurrencies are highly volatile, which means no one can give you a definitive picture of what to expect. We must hold on to this truth from the start to remain alert as you trade and invest: the market can rise as high as it can and fall below your expectations. Savvy investors stay prepared by expecting the best while preparing for the worst.

However, through observations, analysis, and expert insights into the bitcoin's nature today, we can share some possibilities for bitcoin's future. These are the projections by the world's top bitcoin experts, and we agree with their analysis because one thing is sure; Bitcoin will remain relevant in the future.

Bitcoin might face a series of regulatory threats.
Although bitcoin will rise and gain prominence as the currency of choice for investors, regulatory threats may also strangle it. Countries that seek to protect their fiat from cryptocurrencies will come up with all kinds of laws to stifle the continued use of cryptocurrencies.

Countries like Nigeria and India are already cracking down on bitcoin, and the big question is, "what if the rest of the world follows suit?" Most experts argue that the answer lies in the fact that the world is fluid, and it is easy to carry out business with bitcoin in other countries.

While experts insist that prohibitions and regulations will not be effective, you should know that rules can restrict ease of investment with bitcoins in countries where bitcoins are banned. Pay attention to the laws enacted in your country of residence regarding cryptocurrency, as this serves as a guide as you invest.

- **More businesses (online and offline) will accept Bitcoin as a payment gateway**.

This prediction is one a more significant percentage of bitcoin and crypto experts agree on based on the current happenings in the cryptocurrency sector. Ass the number of users increases, more and more businesses will start to accept bitcoin as a payment gateway.

The law of demand and supply will make this prediction happen in the future: the demand for bitcoin will skyrocket, and supply will be enabled through sales, purchases, and exchanges.

- **Bitcoin may become the internet's reserve currency**.

Some experts still argue and doubt the possibility of bitcoin being the global reserve currency, but they are very optimistic about bitcoin becoming the internet's reserve currency.

It is expected that bitcoin will evolve and become the internet's natural currency in the future, such that E-commerce becomes an increasingly viable venture. Most e-commerce merchants are already pivoting to bitcoin payments to capture a more global audience, creating a ripple effect in the future.

- **Bitcoin and fiat will be used side by side**.

This prediction is quite an interesting one because already, we use bitcoin side by side with fiat: people can buy and sell bitcoin with fiat and vice versa. However, there is so much certainty about the future that this will be at a heightened level.

Experts agree that bitcoin will no longer play a "supportive" role in the future. Instead, bitcoin will be used for varying services through the DIRECT exchange by a more significant percentage of users than what is obtainable today. Imagine a world where the dollar and bitcoin can be used simultaneously: fantastic!!

- **Increased threat and increased security**

Despite the certainty bitcoin users have in terms of security and how difficult it is to hack the blockchain, threats still exist. More so, as bitcoin increases in value, these threats will also increase hence the reason experts have warned bitcoin holders to ensure they keep their wallets safe. In the future, bitcoin will remain safe, but since threats will increase, investors must be intentional with heightened security.

On the flip side, as threats increase, bitcoin security will also be strengthened to mitigate the threats and minimize risks. Now we have the 2-factor authentication, but there will be more robust security measures in place as threats arise in the future.

- **New users and venture funds**

With the coronavirus pandemic outbreak, the bitcoin market witnessed an influx of new users who poured in to maximize its value. The new users also contributed to making the price of bitcoin hit the roof as institutional investors reinvested in Bitcoin.

Despite the uncertainties in the financial market, Bitcoin is rated as a "hedging tool" and may remain the same in the future as people use it to diversify their investment portfolio.

- **The currency of choice of international trade?**

Some experts have projected that cryptocurrencies will become the currency of choice for international trade, and bitcoin is at the center of this expectation. PayPal (PYPL) and Tesla (TSLA) have made investments into cryptocurrencies, with Tesla buying $1.5 billion in Bitcoin.

With Tesla and PayPal making such moves, it is safe to predict that people can get paid for services or receive funds on PayPal through bitcoin. Tesla CEO Elon Musk has also not ruled out the possibility of accepting bitcoin for a car payment.

Bitcoin is safe, has very fast transaction timelines, and can be accepted in any country with cryptocurrencies. If countries do not keep up with their regulatory threats, bitcoin will thrive, and it could become the currency for international trade.

The future of Bitcoin is unarguably very bright. There may be bumps for investors and traders, but it doesn't change the fact that Bitcoin is becoming a regular part of our financial reality.

From the trends and insights shared above, it is evident that whatever investments you make now with bitcoin will yield more significant results (if you are patient). Many years ago, when bitcoin first launched, some people didn't invest in it because they assumed that the world wasn't ready for digital currencies. Well, here we are today with lots of newcomers into the bitcoin space and people making a fortune from it.

To avoid becoming like those with regrets about not keying in early enough into the bitcoin market, you've got to start now to secure the future. There are lots of lessons to be learned as you trade today, which will help you in the future, but first, you've got to start with purchasing your first cryptocurrencies.

Chapter 7

The 10 SECRETS TO

SUCCESS IN BITCOIN

How to achieve success with Bitcoin

In this guide, we will give you a summary of the 10 secrets to success in Bitcoin investing.

You have probably already heard something about Bitcoin or cryptocurrencies in general. You are impressed by the massive growth this exciting technology is experiencing— but where do you begin?

You may be wanting to enter the cryptocurrency market but are having doubts. You may also be thinking that all the good opportunities have already passed you by.

However, in my opinion, it's never too late. In fact, I will now cover the key to success when investing in Bitcoin. Think of it a bit like being right back at the beginning of the web in the 90s—this Blockchain technology certainly has a bright future ahead of it.

1. Become an expert in cryptocurrency technology

We firmly believe that good things always start with a proper education. With this in mind, if you would like to be a successful BITCOIN investor, you initially need to invest your time upfront to learn all there is to know about this exciting but complex field.

Moreover, you would be very wise to take an online training course in technical analysis or Bitcoin programming languages.

We know that this cryptocurrency technology is very novel and has the potential to act as a disruptive force. So, you should learn all aspects of it—starting with reading the Bitcoin Whitepaper.

Other famous subjects include Bitcoin mining, which can be divided into the following categories:

- Proof of work (Wikipedia here)
- Proof of stake (Wikipedia here)

You will certainly be rewarded if you do your own research (DYOR) and know something about those things listed above. This will set you on the proper path of finding a successful strategy as a budding cryptocurrency investor.

2. Only spend money you don't need in the near future

Whenever we think about investing, we always want to find the right opportunities that come with low risk and high reward. When doing this, you need to make sure you don't get into a financial crisis.

However, that being said, invest only what you can afford to lose—and expect that this might very well happen to you.

You should also think about your mindset and the impact on FOMO by taking profits way too early!

Investing should never be about finding the simplest way to pay your monthly rent or other expenses. Rather, it is a vehicle to accumulate wealth over a long time period.

Bitcoin has been around for nearly a decade and is here to stay. It has a bright future ahead of it!

3. Planning for boom and bust periods

When investing in cryptocurrency, you must learn to cope with pimp-n-dump coins, crypto scams, and whales trying to govern cryptocurrency markets. In fact, it is all part of the sport—and can even making investing in this asset very exciting.

The Bitcoin markets are still very young and, this sort of decentralized technology has disrupted the typical centralized governance or regulation. We could even go as far as to say that this is often the biggest reason for the success of Bitcoin.

Specifically, its decentralized nature is the main reason that big corporations haven't entered this space yet. As I explained earlier, investing in crypto might seem like a big risk, but at the same time, big profits are ripe for the taking. We think the sky is the limit here!

Bitcoin investing using the Wall Street Cheat Sheet

We want to give you the Wall Street cheat sheet to Bitcoin investing.

To start seeing profits as a cryptocurrency investor, you need to know the boom-bust cycles. Period.

For instance, if you're feeling euphoric and as if you could take on the world—be careful not to act in a rash manner. This feeling won't last forever. Instead, in moments such as these, it's better to gratefully pocket the profits.

In contrast, if the cryptocurrency markets turn against you, you could end up with heavy losses or seriously in the red for an awfully very long time. At times such as these, many investors often sell out of fear and run away, or instead, they may be angry and feel depressed. However, with the Wall Street Cheat Sheet, you can feel empowered to make the right decision in terms of purchasing new assets.

4. Diversification—The key to success in Bitcoin markets

The key to the success that underpins cryptocurrencies and the associated disruptive blockchain technology comes from their innovative founder, Satoshi Nakamoto.

The number one rule when investing in cryptocurrency assets is to not get too emotionally attached or involved. You need to remember that as an investor, you are simply an outsider. So, set in your mind that your money comes first!

Also, never back one horse—instead, put your money into several different assets. Investing means there are going to be losses. Simply put, you can't be right 100% of the time. Therefore, know that you will not get the expected results for your investments all the time. However, you can put yourself in a stronger position if you back sound investments in the first place.

In my opinion, when investing in cryptocurrency or Bitcoin, always keep a certain amount in the mother of all coins—BTC.

5. Always have a concept and ensure specialization

For any investor, it's vital to possess a sound plan that can be reactive to changes in the market before putting your money into Bitcoin or other cryptocurrencies.

Maybe you assume that investing in crypto will get you rich overnight. If so, then, unfortunately, I've got to disappoint you. It just doesn't work that way!

Instead, being a profitable investor means you've got to religiously check your figures and be patient. In fact, the key to success with investing in cryptocurrency is to play the long game.

Secret to success in Bitcoin in 2030

With that being said, it just takes time. So, to avoid getting distracted or feeling overwhelmed, it's very wise have a transparent end goal or target in place from the off.

Investing in Bitcoin could even be a ticket out of 9-5 wage slavery and set you on a path to financial freedom. Always remember your goals!

6. Find out how to try and do proper altcoin Reviews

If you visit the Coinmarketcap website, you'll be able to see that the amount of altcoin projects is pretty huge. In fact, new ones are shooting up constantly.

So, what is the best way to find the hidden gems in among all of these altcoins?

The first thing you should be looking to do is to go check out their base code on Github. By doing this, you will be able to learn some proper coding skills (see point 1). If, for instance, their base code is private or doesn't have recent comments, then the project or altcoin is an immediate red flag.

How to reach Bitcoin with proper research
Other stuff you could check for is as follows:

- The size of the community
- How active it is on Reddit

- On which percentage exchanges that is altcoin listed
- What marketing strategy is being used

To summarize, finding the simplest altcoins takes time but it will be very rewarding!

Secret to success with cryptocurrency and altcoins

7. Keep it simple—Stick with one or just some cryptocurrency exchanges

Besides the thousands of altcoin projects out there, you will also notice that there is an overwhelming number of cryptocurrency exchanges. For example, when visiting the Coinmarketcap website, you might notice the large number of exchanges.

The best advice is to stick with the exchanges with the very best volumes first. When you gain more confidence with a few particular ones, you can try the smaller ones too. The following exchanges are highly regarded among cryptocurrency investors:

- Binance
- Coinbase
- Coinmama
- Coinswitch

8. Be able to handle the volatility—This is another secret to success

The cryptocurrency markets are feared and loved at the same time due to their high volatility.

Once you enter these unregulated markets, it's very important to be very patient and take a protracted term mindset (see point 5). In fact, the key to success in the cryptocurrency markets is having the ability to just sit down on your hands for a spectacularly long time. Patience will always be rewarded.

It is important to know that the cryptocurrency markets are in accumulation phase for much of the time, rather than being volatile on a daily basis.

Dogecoin accumulation and pump
Dogecoin earlier in 2021

9. Know what it appears like to HODL

The previous discussion shows you how patience will always be rewarded.

However, to be a profitable cryptocurrency investor in the long run, you must hold on for dear life (HODL) to many of your crypto assets. Yes, the important secret to success with Bitcoin is having the ability to HODL.

Notably, all Bitcoin investors who are successful nowadays have been holding on to Bitcoin for nearly a decade now. By doing this, profits on the scale of 100x, 1000x, or perhaps even 10000x are possible as your reward. So, what's the simplest way to do this? In my opinion, you must store a minimum of 30% of your Bitcoin investments offline in cold storage.

10. Find like-minded individuals

This is one of the famous quotes for successful millionaires from the hugely influential book called The Intelligent Investor. The key to success comes from surrounding yourself with like-minded people or investors. This also goes for investing with Bitcoin.

Of course, you shouldn't just eliminate your old friends overnight. However, it's very wise to find some real crypto OGs who already know the best way to play this game. But where can you find them? Most of the famous people within the crypto industry have accounts on Twitter, so to get informed, definitely start there. Also, other social media channels such as Telegram, Slack, or Discord will do a pretty good job too!

With this guidance, you can confidently dive into the cryptocurrency market, buy your first Bitcoin (and other coins), and start investing. We live in exciting times where digital currencies are taking over. Therefore, this is the BEST time to leverage the boom and secure your financial future today.

Conclusion

Well done!! You have done an excellent job at reading this practical guide which is a testament to your commitment to maximizing cryptocurrencies' economic power. We learned how to buy bitcoin and understand how exchanges work, and unraveled insights into bitcoin security.

We also considered current trends in the cryptocurrency market and the concept of mining and rounded up with ideas on the future of Bitcoin. You have a complete package for a practical guide with pictures for direction, and with this, you can confidently get into the cryptocurrency market ready to win. Regardless of what the future holds for the finance sector, one thing is sure: cryptocurrencies are here to stay.

We have achieved a massive milestone with this material, but this is only the beginning because now you know the potentials Bitcoin has, you also need to make a move.

Knowing what to do is good but doing it and keep at it until you get the results you seek is even better.

Some people get to the "concluding" part of a book and feel, "oh yes, we are at the end, so now I can drop this book and move on to the next." Doing this with every book you read means you would "know" so much about many different opportunities but very few results. You haven't come this far to get little results now, have you? You read the first book, and now this one shows your willingness to capitalize on the digital currency trend and make a fortune from it.

Your reading and learning efforts should match your commitment to act on the information you received: this is how you gain the actual value.

The cryptocurrency market will constantly evolve, which means those who earn from it keep their eyes close to the market.

You can only remain close to the market when you are actively involved with your crypto coins: trading, buying, selling, investing, holding, etc. Today, so many people know the potentials that cryptocurrencies have, but that is a much more significant percentage than those making gains from the market.

While I applaud your commitment to reading, I would also like to use this concluding section as a call to action, reminding you that the most important lessons you will learn are from being active in the market.

The crypto market remains a volatile one (this is a hard truth but one you must accept). So, you will win sometimes and lose sometimes; it's all a part of the process: but one thing is sure, you will LEARN! As you learn, you will get used to the investment process; you will understand the market more, know how the exchanges

work, and even predict trends.

Be proactive, dedicated, and committed to knowing more about cryptocurrencies, and you will never be left behind.

Remember all you learned in the chapters and sections above, practice by entering the market with disposable cash and gradually build a substantial cryptocurrency investment portfolio.

If you enjoyed this book

please let me know your thoughts by

leaving a short review on amazon. Thank you

CLICK ON THE IMAGE TO DOWNLOAD 2 BOOKS IN 1 TODAY